# Happiness Walks on Busy Feet

Compiled by Vernon McLellan

Great Quotations Publishing

Published by Great Quotations Publishing.
1967 Quincy Ct., Glendale Heights, Illinois 60139

ISBN 1-56245-059-X

Printed in the United States of America.

Happiness is the result of being too busy
to be miserable.

The roots of happiness grow deepest
in the soil of service.

Happiness is feeling good about yourself.

Happiness is something that comes into our
lives through a door we don't
remember leaving open.

The secret of happiness is to
count your blessings while others
are adding up their troubles.

Happiness is . . .
the smell of bread baking.

All our guests bring us happiness —
some in coming, some in going.

The really happy man is the one
who can enjoy the scenery when
he has to take a detour.

The secret of happy living is not to do what
you like but to like what you do.

Happiness is not the absence of conflict but
the ability to cope with it.

Happiness is like jam — you can't spread even a little without getting some on yourself.

Happiness consists in activity. It's a
running stream, not a stagnant pool.

The thing that counts the most in the pursuit
of happiness is choosing the right traveling
companion.

All who want happiness must be willing to
share it.

Happiness is a positive cash flow.

Happiness is the art of making a bouquet of
those flowers within reach.

In the pursuit of happiness, the difficulty lies
in knowing when you have caught up.

*R.H. Grenville*

Happiness is . . .
the sight of a sleeping child.

Most people are about as happy as they
make up their minds to be.

*Abraham Lincoln*

Happiness is . . .
your first love.

Happiness is . . .
the first robin of spring.

Happiness is often where you least expect it.

Happiness increases the more
you spread it around.

The grand essentials for happiness are:
something to do, something to love and
something to hope for.

*Chalmers*

Happiness is being too sick to go to school,
but not too sick to watch television.

Some people cause happiness where they go
— others, when.

The road to happiness is under construction.

Happiness is . . .
a perfect rose.

Happiness is . . .
sunshine after a shower.

Happiness is . . .
the child of loving parents.

Happiness is . . .
chocolate cake.

Happiness is . . .
puppies.

Happiness makes up in height for what it
lacks in length.

*Robert Frost*

Happiness is the delicate balance between
what one is and what one has.

*F.H. Denison*

Happiness is the feeling you're feeling when you want to keep on feeling it.

The U.S. Constitution doesn't guarantee happiness, only the pursuit of it. You have to catch up with it yourself.

*Benjamin Franklin*

It isn't our position but our disposition that
makes us happy.

Happiness is a direction not a destination.

Success is getting what you want; happiness
is wanting what you get.

Happiness is . . .
hotdogs at the ballpark.

Happiness is . . .
the smile of a child.

Nowadays every man wants life, liberty,
and a new automobile in
which to pursue happiness.

The surest path to happiness is in losing
yourself in a cause greater than yourself.

The only ones among you who will be really
happy are those who will have sought and
found how to serve.

*Albert Schweitzer*

For every minute you're angry, you lose sixty
seconds of happiness.

Happiness is . . .

sitting in front of a fireplace
on a cold winter night.

He who forgets the language of gratitude can never be on speaking terms with happiness.

Pursuing happiness would be a lot easier if
everybody slowed down a little.

Happiness consists of living each day as if it
were the first day of your honeymoon and
the last day of your vacation.

Happiness is home-brewed.

A small house will hold as much happiness
as a big one.

Real happiness is going to a high school
class reunion and learning that the boy who
was voted most likely to succeed — didn't.

Happiness is a place somewhere between too much and too little.

A man has happiness in the palm of his hands if he can fill his days with real work and his nights with real rest.

Happiness is like the common cold —
it's catching!

True happiness may be sought, thought or
caught — but never bought.

Happiness is discovering that the
slip of paper under your windshield
is just an advertisement.

The heart is happiest when
it beats for others.

The happiest people are those who are too busy to notice whether they are happy or not.

Happiness is like a potato salad — when shared with others, it's a picnic.

Happiness is getting something you wanted
but didn't expect.

Happiness is learning that your daughter's
boyfriend has had his electric guitar
repossessed by the finance company.

You'll be happier if you'll give people a bit of your heart rather than a piece of your mind.

Happiness adds and multiplies as we
divide it with others.

When happiness gets into your system, it is
bound to break out on your face.

Prudence keeps life safe,
but does not often make it happy.

*Samuel Johnson*

Do something every day to make other
people happy, even if it's only
to leave them alone.

Some pursue happiness — others create it.

Happiness is a thing to be
practiced, like the violin.

*John Lubbock*

Happiness is . . .
walking on the beach.

Happiness is not perfected until it is shared.

Happiness is hiring a baby-sitter
who is on a diet.

The happiest people are those who discover
that what they should be doing and what
they are doing are the same thing.

The miserable man is unhappy every day;
but the cheerful man enjoys a constant feast.

Happiness is pursuing something but not
catching it — except chasing
a bus on a rainy night.

Happiness is having a scratch for every itch.

*Ogden Nash*

Happiness is . . .
sleeping late.

Happiness is . . .
found money.

A happy life is one spent in learning,
earning and yearning.

*Lillian Gish*

The secret of a happy life
is to accept change gracefully.

*James Stewart*

The optimist is often as wrong as the
pessimist; but he is far happier.

Happiness is . . .
seeing a beautiful bride.

My life has no purpose, no direction, no aim, no meaning, and yet I'm happy. I can't figure it out. What am I doing right?

Happiness is not being pained in body or
troubled in mind.

*Thomas Jefferson*

The secret of happiness is this: Let your interests be as wide as possible, and let your reactions to the things and persons that interest you be as far as possible friendly rather than hostile.

*Bertrand Russell*

Happiness is a way station between
too little and too much.

*Channing Pollock*

A person is never happy except at
the price of some ignorance.

*Anatole France*

Happiness is . . .
a perfect sand castle.

The formula for complete happiness is to be very busy with the unimportant.

*A. Edward Newton*

All happiness depends on
a leisurely breakfast.

*John Gunther*

Happiness is . . .
a hot air balloon ride.

Happiness is a stock that doubles in a year.

*Ira U. Cobleigh*

Happiness? That's nothing more than health
and a poor memory.

*Albert Scweitzer*

There is nothing which has yet been
contrived by man by which so much
happiness is produced as by a good tavern.

*Samuel Johnson (1709 - 1784)*

Happiness is . . .
doing a good deed anonymously

If happiness truly consisted in physical ease
and freedom from care, then the
happiest individual would not be either
a man or a woman; it would be,
I think, an American cow.

*William Lyon Phelps*

What everyone wants from life is continuous
and genuine happiness. Happiness is the
rational understanding of life and the world.

*Baruch Spinoza*

The happiest man is he who learns from nature the lesson of worship.

*Ralph Waldo Emerson (1803 - 1882)*

Happiness is . . .

flowers from the right person.

If a man has important work, and enough
leisure and income to enable him to do it
properly, he is in possession of as much
happiness as is good for any of
the children of Adam.

*R. H. Tawney*

What can be added to the happiness of a
man who is in health, out of debt,
and has a clear conscience?

*Adam Smith (1723 - 1790)*

The happy do not believe in miracles.

*Johann W. von Goethe (1749 - 1832)*

What a wonderful life I've had! I only wish
I'd realized it sooner.

Happiness is not a state to arrive at, but a manner of traveling.

*Margaret Lee Runbeck*

Happiness is . . .
a beautiful sunset.

Once you have heard the lark, known the swish of feet through hill-top grass and smelt the earth made ready for the seed, you are never again going to be fully happy about the cities and towns that man carries like a crippling weight upon his back.

*Gwyn Thomas*

Many people are extremely happy, but are absolutely worthless to society.

*Charles Gow*

Happiness is the only sanction of life; where
happiness fails, existence remains a mad
and lamentable experiment.

*George Santayana*

Most of us believe in trying to make other
people happy only if they can be happy in
ways which we approve.

*Robert S. Lynd*

Happiness is . . .
being part of a team.

The only power a god can teach is the power
of doing without happiness.

*George Bernard Shaw*

The greatest happiness you can have is
knowing that you do not
necessarily require happiness.

*William Saroyan*

There is no greater sorrow than to recall, in misery, the time when we were happy.

*Dante Alighieri (1265 - 1321)*

No greater grief than to remember days of
gladness when sorrow is at hand.

*Friedrich Schiller (1729 - 1805)*

How many things are there
which I do not want.

*Socrates (470? - 390 B.C.)*

To be without some of the things you want is
an indispensable part of happiness.

*Bertrand Russell*

Happy the man who early learns the wide
chasm that lies between his wishes and his
powers!

*Johann W. von Goethe (1749 - 1832)*

Man, unlike the animals, has never learned
that the sole purpose of life is to enjoy it.

*Samuel Butler*

I have diligently numbered the days of pure and genuine happiness which have fallen to my lot: they amount to fourteen.

*Abd-El-Raham (912 - 961)*

Happiness is . . .
the last day of your diet.

Happiness is . . .
sailing on a clear day.

The pursuit of happiness is a most
ridiculous phrase: if you pursue
happiness you'll never find it.

*C. P. Snow*

One of the indictments of civilizations is that
happiness and intelligence are so
rarely found in the same person.

*William Feather*

The main thing needed to make
men happy is intelligence.

*Bertrand Russell*

The great pleasure in life is doing what
people say you cannot do.

*Walker Bagehot (1826 - 1877)*

Pleasure is the only thing to live for.
Nothing ages like happiness.

*Oscar Wilde (1854 - 1900)*

Happiness is . . .
finishing on time.

Joys are our wings.

It takes life to love life.

*Edgar Lee Masters*

Happiness resides not in possessions
and not in gold; the feeling of happiness
dwells in the soul.

*Democritus*

Very little is needed to make a happy life. It is all within yourself, in your way of thinking.

*Marcus Aurelius*

Men can only be happy when they do not
assume that the object of life is happiness.

*George Orwell*

Be happy. It's one way of being wise.

*Colette*

To love is to place our happiness in
the happiness of another.

*G. W. von Leibnitz*

The sense of existence is
the greatest happiness.

*Benjamin Disraeli*

Happiness is an inside job.

The supreme happiness of life
is the conviction of being loved for yourself,
or, more correctly, being loved
in spite of yourself.

*Victor Hugo*

If only we'd stop trying to be happy, we
could have a pretty good time.

Happiness is . . .

finding exactly what you were looking for.

A happy life has few regrets.

Happiness is fun and food . . .
Kodachromed for later view.

*Maryna Mannes*

The moments of happiness we enjoy take us
by surprise. It is not that we seize them,
but that they seize us.

*Ashley Montagu*

Happiness is . . .

peace.

Happiness always looks small while you hold
it in your hands, but let it go, and you learn
at once how big and precious it is.

*Maxim Gorky*

Real happiness is cheap enough, yet how
dearly we pay for its counterfeit.

*Hosea Ballou*

The best way to secure future happiness is to be as happy as is rightfully possible today.

*Charles W. Eliot*

Happiness is a habit — cultivate it.

*Elbert Hubbard*

It's pretty hard to tell what does bring
happiness. Poverty an' wealth
have both failed.

*Kin Hubbard*

Happiness is not a reward —
it is a consequence.
Suffering is not a punishment — is is a result.

*Robert G. Ingersoll*

Happiness is the legal tender of the soul.

The rays of happiness, like those of light, are colorless when unbroken.

*Henry Wadsworth Longfellow*

The foolish man seeks happiness in the distance; The wise grows it under his feet.

*James Oppenheim*

Happiness to me is wine,
Effervescent, superfine.
Full of tang and fiery pleasure,
Far too hot to leave me leisure
For a single thought beyond it.

*Amy Lowell*

It is wrong to assume that men of immense
wealth are always happy.

*John D. Rockefeller*

Happiness is . . .
a job well done.

Happiness grows at our own firesides, and is
not to be picked in strangers' gardens.

*Douglas Jerrould*

Happiness is the interval
between periods of unhappiness.

*Don Marquis*

Happiness is . . .
spending time with your grandparents.

Good friends, good books and a sleepy
conscience: this is the ideal life.

*Mark Twain*

Happiness lies in the taste, and not in the things; and it is from having what we desire that we are happy - not from having what others think desirable.

*Duc de La Rochefoucauld*

The only really happy fold are married
women and single men.

*H. L. Mencken*

Wandering seemed no more than the
happiness of an anxious man.

*Albert Camus*

Happiness is the natural flower of duty.

*Phillips Brooks*

Happiness is . . .
catching the biggest fish.

Whoever is happy will make others happy
too. He who has courage and faith
will never perish in misery.

*Ann Frank*

Happiness is . . .
doing the right thing.